Dear Parent,

A good foundation of math skills will help your child throughout his or her life. That's why it's important for kids to develop this foundation at a young age. This book uses fun and interesting activities to help reinforce your child's addition skills. Kids will love the zany puzzles, games, and pictures. Follow these simple steps to make the most of this book:

- Find a comfortable place where you and your child can work quietly together.
- Encourage your child to go at his or her own pace.
- Help your child with the problems if he or she needs it.
- Offer lots of praise and support.
- Let your child reward his or her work with the included stickers.
- Most of all, remember that learning should be fun! Take time to look at the pictures, laugh at the funny characters, and enjoy this special time spent together.

Baby Birds

Add the numbers. Write your answers in the eggs.

1.
$$3 + 2 = 5$$

2.
$$1 + 3 = 4$$

3.
$$4 + 2 = 6$$

4.
$$1 + 4 = 5$$

5.
$$2 + 4 = 6$$

6.
$$1 + 2 = 3$$

7.
$$1 + 1 = 2$$

8.
$$3 + 3 = 6$$

Penguins Swim

Penguins are very good swimmers. Add the numbers to take a dive.

1.
$$\begin{array}{r} 6 \\ +\,3 \\ \hline 9 \end{array}$$

2.
$$\begin{array}{r} 5 \\ +\,1 \\ \hline 6 \end{array}$$

3.
$$\begin{array}{r} 2 \\ +\,6 \\ \hline 8 \end{array}$$

4.
$$\begin{array}{r} 0 \\ +\,6 \\ \hline 6 \end{array}$$

5.
$$\begin{array}{r} 4 \\ +\,0 \\ \hline 4 \end{array}$$

6.
$$\begin{array}{r} 6 \\ +\,1 \\ \hline 7 \end{array}$$

7.
$$\begin{array}{r} 3 \\ +\,1 \\ \hline 4 \end{array}$$

8.
$$\begin{array}{r} 4 \\ +\,4 \\ \hline 8 \end{array}$$

A Penguin Pool

Add the numbers.

1. $\begin{array}{r} 3 \\ +6 \\ \hline \end{array}$

2. $\begin{array}{r} 2 \\ +5 \\ \hline \end{array}$

3. $\begin{array}{r} 4 \\ +4 \\ \hline \end{array}$

4. $\begin{array}{r} 6 \\ +1 \\ \hline \end{array}$

5. $\begin{array}{r} 1 \\ +5 \\ \hline \end{array}$

6. $\begin{array}{r} 4 \\ +0 \\ \hline \end{array}$

7. $\begin{array}{r} 1 \\ +4 \\ \hline \end{array}$

8. $\begin{array}{r} 3 \\ +3 \\ \hline \end{array}$

A Penguin Party!

Add the number each group of penguins. Write the answers on the line aw a line from each answer to the m ing number in the box.

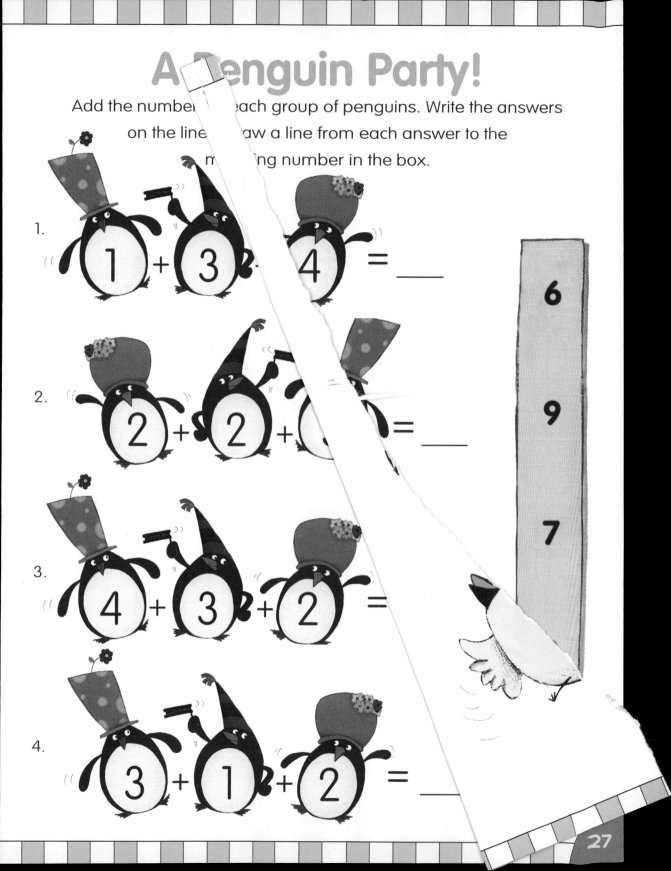

1. 1 + 3 + 4 = ___

2. 2 + 2 + ___ = ___

3. 4 + 3 + 2 = ___

4. 3 + 1 + 2 = ___

6

9

7

Baby Horses

Baby horses are much smaller than adult horses.
Add these numbers and circle the smallest number.

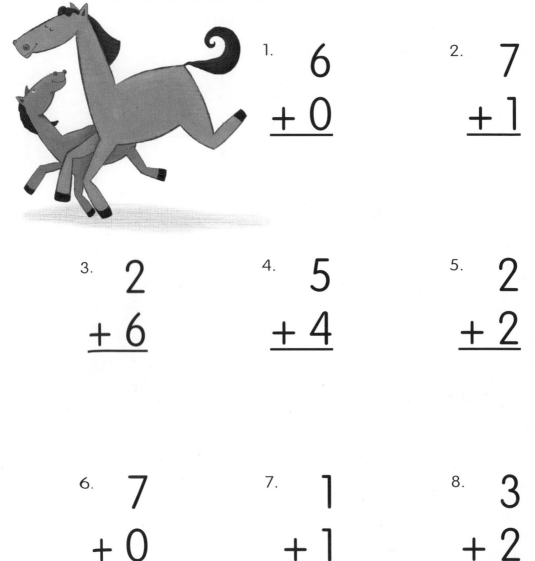

1.
$$\begin{array}{r} 6 \\ + 0 \\ \hline \end{array}$$

2.
$$\begin{array}{r} 7 \\ + 1 \\ \hline \end{array}$$

3.
$$\begin{array}{r} 2 \\ + 6 \\ \hline \end{array}$$

4.
$$\begin{array}{r} 5 \\ + 4 \\ \hline \end{array}$$

5.
$$\begin{array}{r} 2 \\ + 2 \\ \hline \end{array}$$

6.
$$\begin{array}{r} 7 \\ + 0 \\ \hline \end{array}$$

7.
$$\begin{array}{r} 1 \\ + 1 \\ \hline \end{array}$$

8.
$$\begin{array}{r} 3 \\ + 2 \\ \hline \end{array}$$

Growing Up

Add the numbers. Write the answers on the baby horses.
Then draw a line between each baby horse and the adult
horse showing the same number.

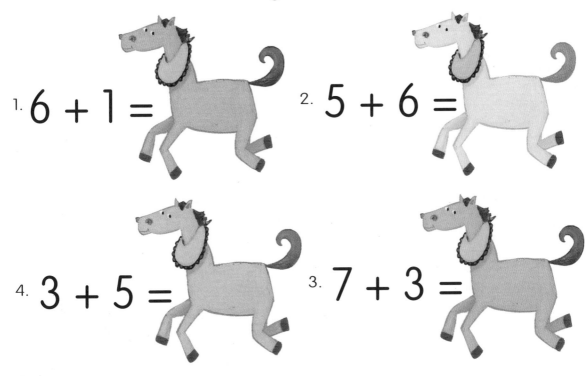

1. $6 + 1 =$

2. $5 + 6 =$

4. $3 + 5 =$

3. $7 + 3 =$

11   7   10   8

Horsing Around

Add the numbers for some fun with farm animals.

1.
$$\begin{array}{r} 6 \\ +\ 4 \\ \hline \end{array}$$

2.
$$\begin{array}{r} 5 \\ +\ 1 \\ \hline \end{array}$$

3.
$$\begin{array}{r} 3 \\ +\ 7 \\ \hline \end{array}$$

4.
$$\begin{array}{r} 5 \\ +\ 6 \\ \hline \end{array}$$

5.
$$\begin{array}{r} 7 \\ +\ 3 \\ \hline \end{array}$$

6.
$$\begin{array}{r} 9 \\ +\ 2 \\ \hline \end{array}$$

7.
$$\begin{array}{r} 3 \\ +\ 5 \\ \hline \end{array}$$

1. $\begin{array}{r} 7 \\ +1 \\ \hline \end{array}$

2. $\begin{array}{r} 2 \\ +4 \\ \hline \end{array}$

3. $\begin{array}{r} 6 \\ +0 \\ \hline \end{array}$

4. $\begin{array}{r} 7 \\ +3 \\ \hline \end{array}$

5. $\begin{array}{r} 5 \\ +6 \\ \hline \end{array}$

6. $\begin{array}{r} 8 \\ +2 \\ \hline \end{array}$

7. $\begin{array}{r} 3 \\ +5 \\ \hline \end{array}$

Horse Play

Add the numbers. Draw a line from each
answer to the matching number in the box.

1.
$$\begin{array}{r} 0 \\ + 6 \\ \hline \end{array}$$

2.
$$\begin{array}{r} 3 \\ + 6 \\ \hline \end{array}$$

3.
$$\begin{array}{r} 4 \\ + 3 \\ \hline \end{array}$$

4.
$$\begin{array}{r} 5 \\ + 3 \\ \hline \end{array}$$

5.
$$\begin{array}{r} 3 \\ + 1 \\ \hline \end{array}$$

6.
$$\begin{array}{r} 7 \\ + 3 \\ \hline \end{array}$$

9

6

7

4

8

10

Adult Horses

Add the numbers. Circle the highest number.

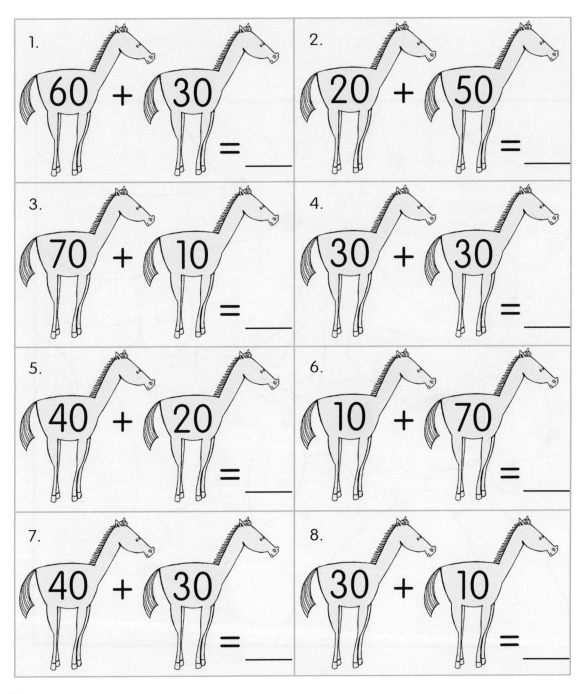

1. 60 + 30 = ___

2. 20 + 50 = ___

3. 70 + 10 = ___

4. 30 + 30 = ___

5. 40 + 20 = ___

6. 10 + 70 = ___

7. 40 + 30 = ___

8. 30 + 10 = ___

Barking Beauties

Color black on the areas that equal 8.

Color brown on the areas that equal 9.

Color blue on the areas that equal 10.

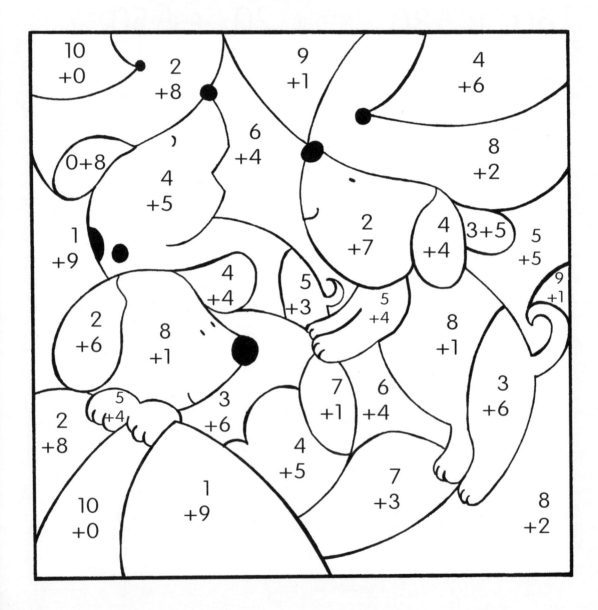

Puppy Love

Puppies grow very fast.

Add the numbers as fast as you can.

1.
$$\begin{array}{r} 12 \\ +14 \\ \hline \end{array}$$

2.
$$\begin{array}{r} 42 \\ +23 \\ \hline \end{array}$$

3.
$$\begin{array}{r} 55 \\ +31 \\ \hline \end{array}$$

4.
$$\begin{array}{r} 24 \\ +34 \\ \hline \end{array}$$

5.
$$\begin{array}{r} 73 \\ +16 \\ \hline \end{array}$$

6.
$$\begin{array}{r} 46 \\ +21 \\ \hline \end{array}$$

7.
$$\begin{array}{r} 35 \\ +52 \\ \hline \end{array}$$

8.
$$\begin{array}{r} 22 \\ +46 \\ \hline \end{array}$$

Paddling Puppies

Add the numbers. Write the answers in the boxes.

1. 63
   +25

2. 34
   +25

3. 83
   +13

4. 52
   +30

5. 66
   +23

6. 23
   +43

7. 58
   +31

8. 64
   +33

Doggie Dance

Add the numbers in each row of dogs.

Draw a line from each answer to the matching number in the box.

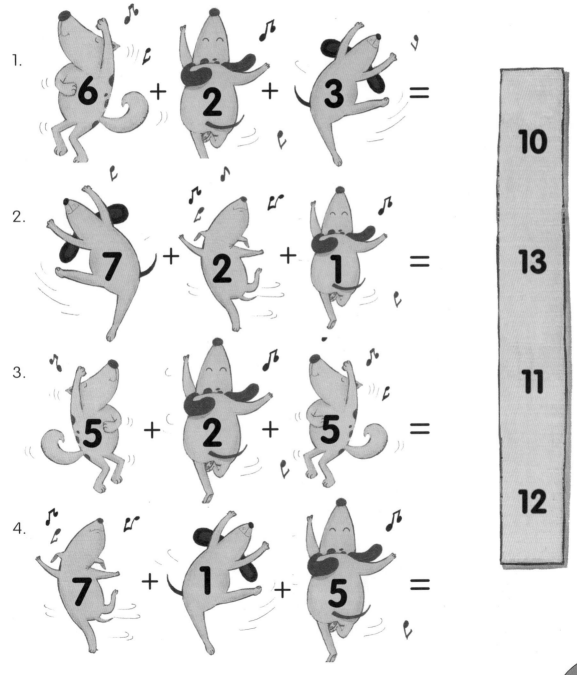

1. $6 + 2 + 3 =$

2. $7 + 2 + 1 =$

3. $5 + 2 + 5 =$

4. $7 + 1 + 5 =$

10

13

11

12

Double the Dogs!

Double each number by adding each number to itself.

1. $7 + \underline{7} = \underline{14}$ ✓

2. $1 + \underline{1} = \underline{2}$ ✓

3. $4 + \underline{4} = \underline{8}$ ✓

4. $5 + \underline{5} = \underline{10}$ ✓

5. $6 + \underline{6} = \underline{12}$ ✓

6. $2 + \underline{2} = \underline{4}$ ✓

7. $3 + \underline{3} = \underline{6}$ ✓

8. $8 + \underline{8} = \underline{16}$ ✓

A Dog Party

Add the numbers.

1.
$$54 + 34 = 88$$

2.
$$21 + 28 = 49$$

3.
$$37 + 41 = 78$$

4.
$$44 + 32 = 76$$

5.
$$51 + 28 = 79$$

6.
$$42 + 12 = 54$$

7.
$$21 + 43 = 64$$

Lion Cub Club

Cubs are baby lions. Count the cubs.

1.

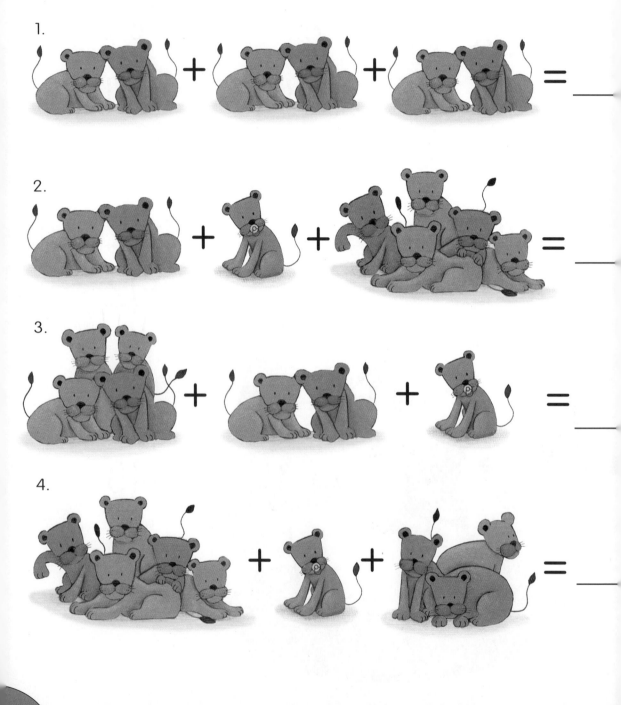

Cute Cubs

Add the numbers. Circle the highest number.

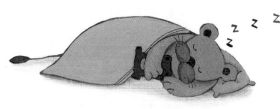

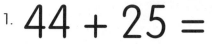

1. 44 + 25 =

2. 71 + 22 = __

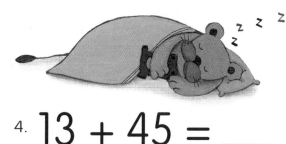

3. 64 + 35 = __

4. 13 + 45 = __

5. 56 + 31 = __

6. 60 + 13 = __

Fun with Cubs

Add the numbers to play.

Circle the highest number.

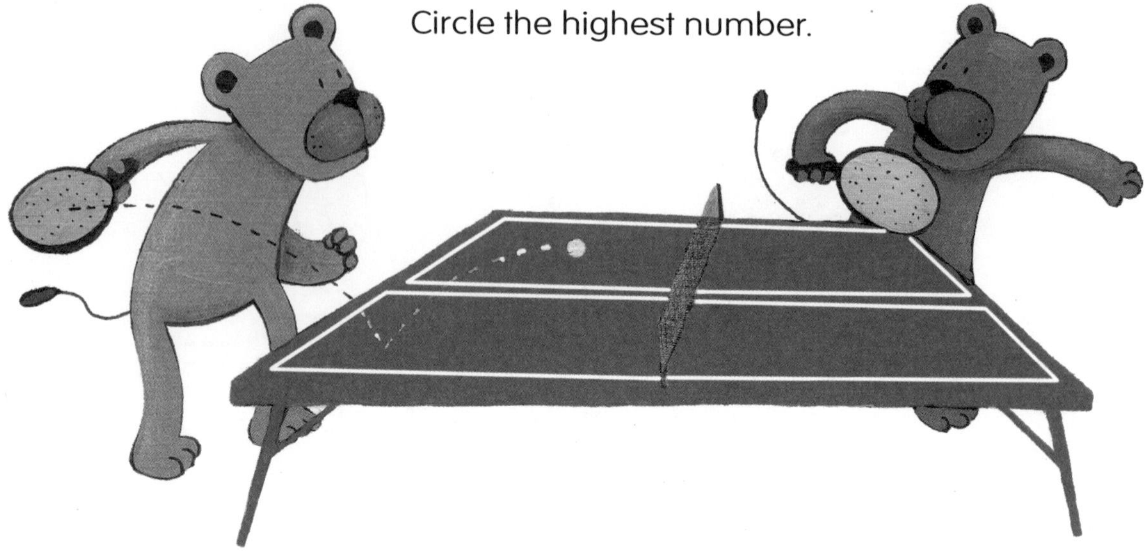

1. 45
   +34

2. 83
   +16

3. 31
   +44

4. 30
   +33

5. 61
   +46

6. 52
   +15

7. 55
   +43

8. 11
   +31

Brian the Lion

1. Brian went to the store to buy a snack. He
   had 35¢ and his mother gave him 12¢ more.
   He also found 10¢ in his piggybank.
   How much money did Brian have? _____

2. Brian went to the store and bought an
   apple, a candy bar, and a pack of gum.
   The apple was 5¢, the candy bar was 7¢,
   and the pack of gum was 4¢.
   How much did Brian spend in the store? _____

Adult Lions

Grown up lions are very big.

Add the numbers and circle the biggest number.

1.
$$\begin{array}{r} 6 \\ +\ 5 \\ \hline \end{array}$$

2.
$$\begin{array}{r} 8 \\ +\ 4 \\ \hline \end{array}$$

3.
$$\begin{array}{r} 7 \\ +\ 7 \\ \hline \end{array}$$

4.
$$\begin{array}{r} 3 \\ +\ 8 \\ \hline \end{array}$$

5.
$$\begin{array}{r} 7 \\ +\ 3 \\ \hline \end{array}$$

6.
$$\begin{array}{r} 5 \\ +\ 7 \\ \hline \end{array}$$

7.
$$\begin{array}{r} 6 \\ +\ 6 \\ \hline \end{array}$$

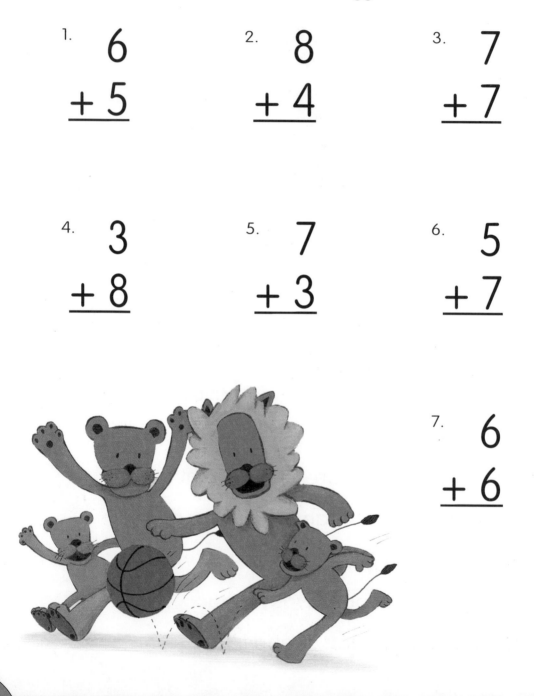

Rip Roarin'

Color orange in the areas that add up to the number 12.

Color brown in the areas that add up to the number 14.

Color green in the areas that add up to the number 16.

Baby Monkeys

Baby monkeys are cute! Add the numbers.

1.
$$4$$
$$+8$$

2.
$$6$$
$$+6$$

3.
$$1$$
$$+9$$

4.
$$7$$
$$+6$$

5.
$$8$$
$$+7$$

6.
$$9$$
$$+5$$

7.
$$6$$
$$+9$$

8.
$$9$$
$$+7$$

Monkey Fun

Add the numbers for some fun with monkeys.

1. $\begin{array}{r} 9 \\ + 3 \\ \hline \end{array}$

2. $\begin{array}{r} 5 \\ + 6 \\ \hline \end{array}$

3. $\begin{array}{r} 8 \\ + 9 \\ \hline \end{array}$

4. $\begin{array}{r} 7 \\ + 6 \\ \hline \end{array}$

5. $\begin{array}{r} 8 \\ + 8 \\ \hline \end{array}$

6. $\begin{array}{r} 9 \\ + 4 \\ \hline \end{array}$

7. $\begin{array}{r} 7 \\ + 3 \\ \hline \end{array}$

8. $\begin{array}{r} 8 \\ + 5 \\ \hline \end{array}$

Funky Monkeys

Add the numbers. Draw a line from each
answer to the matching number on the right.

1. $\begin{array}{r} 7 \\ +7 \\ \hline \end{array}$

2. $\begin{array}{r} 9 \\ +1 \\ \hline \end{array}$

3. $\begin{array}{r} 4 \\ +8 \\ \hline \end{array}$

4. $\begin{array}{r} 8 \\ +5 \\ \hline \end{array}$

5. $\begin{array}{r} 7 \\ +8 \\ \hline \end{array}$

6. $\begin{array}{r} 2 \\ +9 \\ \hline \end{array}$

14

11

10

12

13

15

Count the Monkeys

Add the rows of moneys. Color the group with the biggest number.

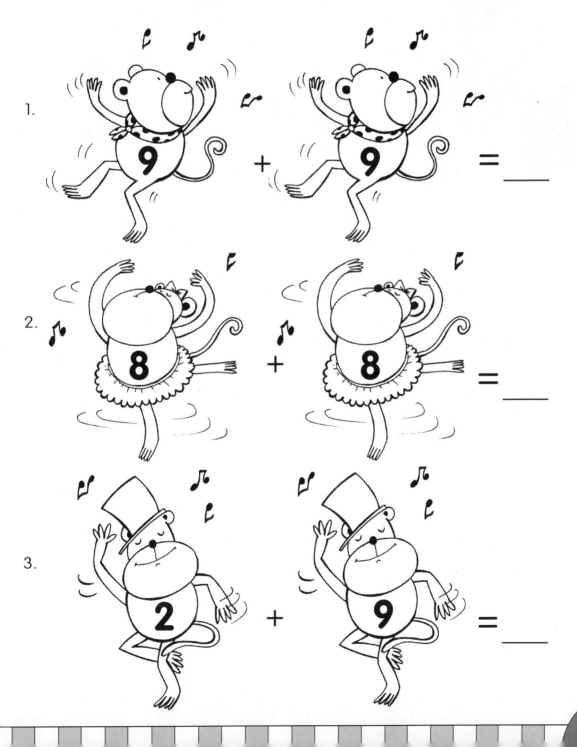

1. $9 + 9 = \underline{\quad}$

2. $8 + 8 = \underline{\quad}$

3. $2 + 9 = \underline{\quad}$

Monkey Magic

Add the numbers to do math magic.

1.
$$\begin{array}{r} 8 \\ + 8 \\ \hline \end{array}$$

2.
$$\begin{array}{r} 9 \\ + 6 \\ \hline \end{array}$$

3.
$$\begin{array}{r} 5 \\ + 7 \\ \hline \end{array}$$

4.
$$\begin{array}{r} 9 \\ + 8 \\ \hline \end{array}$$

5.
$$\begin{array}{r} 7 \\ + 7 \\ \hline \end{array}$$

6.
$$\begin{array}{r} 6 \\ + 5 \\ \hline \end{array}$$

7.
$$\begin{array}{r} 9 \\ + 3 \\ \hline \end{array}$$

8.
$$\begin{array}{r} 6 \\ + 7 \\ \hline \end{array}$$

Mad Monkeys

Add the numbers. Color the picture for some extra fun.

1. 9
   + 4
   ———

2. 5
   + 7
   ———

3. 8
   + 5
   ———

4. 7
   + 8
   ———

5. 6
   + 7
   ———

6. 9
   + 7
   ———

7. 5
   + 5
   ———

8. 9
   + 8
   ———

Baby Mice

Baby mice are tiny.

Add the numbers and circle the smallest number.

1. 8
   +8
   ———

2. 3
   +9
   ———

3. 9
   +5
   ———

4. 7
   +6
   ———

5. 8
   +4
   ———

6. 5
   +5
   ———

7. 7
   +9
   ———

8. 3
   +8
   ———

Litter of Mice

Add the numbers. Draw a line from each answer to the matching mouse.

1.
$$\begin{array}{r} 9 \\ +\,8 \\ \hline \end{array}$$

2.
$$\begin{array}{r} 8 \\ +\,3 \\ \hline \end{array}$$

3.
$$\begin{array}{r} 7 \\ +\,1 \\ \hline \end{array}$$

4.
$$\begin{array}{r} 9 \\ +\,3 \\ \hline \end{array}$$

5.
$$\begin{array}{r} 9 \\ +\,0 \\ \hline \end{array}$$

6.
$$\begin{array}{r} 8 \\ +\,2 \\ \hline \end{array}$$

12

10

8

9

11

17

Dancing Mice

Add the numbers in each row of dancing mice.

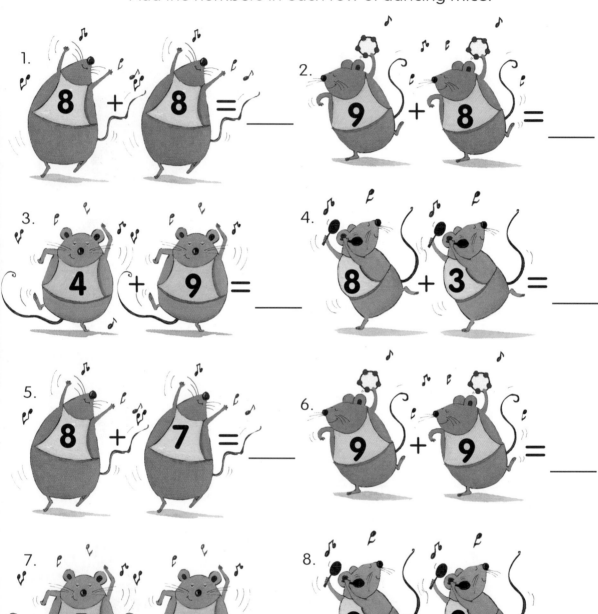

1. 8 + 8 = ___

2. 9 + 8 = ___

3. 4 + 9 = ___

4. 8 + 3 = ___

5. 8 + 7 = ___

6. 9 + 9 = ___

7. 5 + 5 = ___

8. 9 + 2 = ___

Munching Mice

Add the numbers. Write the answers inside the cheese.

1. $2 + 8$

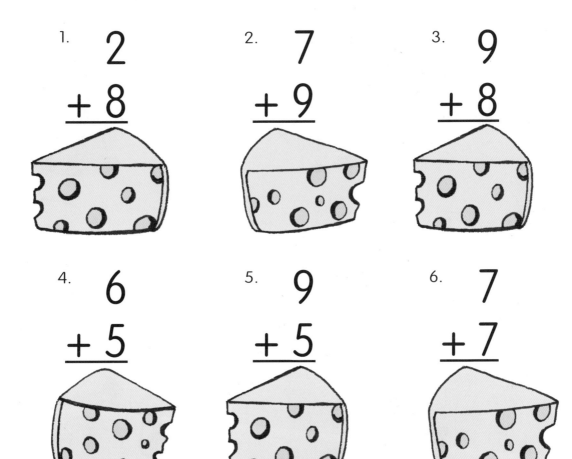

2. $7 + 9$

3. $9 + 8$

4. $6 + 5$

5. $9 + 5$

6. $7 + 7$

Marvelous Mice

Add the numbers. Write the answers in the party hats.

1. $6 + 8 =$

2. $9 + 9 =$

3. $9 + 8 =$

4. $8 + 7 =$

5. $7 + 4 =$

6. $9 + 3 =$

7. $6 + 7 =$

8. $3 + 8 =$

Happy Critters

Add the numbers.

1. 9
    +9

2. 5
    +7

3. 2
    +9

4. 6
    +7

5. 9
    +3

6. 4
    +9

7. 7
    +3

8. 8
    +6

Baby Bears

Add the numbers. Draw a line from each
answer to the matching number in the box.

11

25

12

45

38

57

1. 24
+21

2. 4
+ 7

3. 31
+26

4. 2
+10

5. 16
+22

6. 10
+15

Small and Fuzzy

Baby bears are small and fuzzy.

Add the numbers and circle the smallest number.

1. $\begin{array}{r} 8 \\ +4 \\ \hline \end{array}$

2. $\begin{array}{r} 6 \\ +5 \\ \hline \end{array}$

3. $\begin{array}{r} 7 \\ +6 \\ \hline \end{array}$

4. $\begin{array}{r} 8 \\ +5 \\ \hline \end{array}$

5. $\begin{array}{r} 8 \\ +8 \\ \hline \end{array}$

6. $\begin{array}{r} 6 \\ +7 \\ \hline \end{array}$

7. $\begin{array}{r} 9 \\ +7 \\ \hline \end{array}$

8. $\begin{array}{r} 2 \\ +8 \\ \hline \end{array}$

A Bear Fair

Add the numbers to take a ride.

1. $\begin{array}{r} 9 \\ +9 \\ \hline \end{array}$ 8 x 6 =

2. $\begin{array}{r} 7 \\ +4 \\ \hline \end{array}$ 1 x 1 =

3. $\begin{array}{r} 8 \\ +8 \\ \hline \end{array}$

4. $\begin{array}{r} 5 \\ +7 \\ \hline \end{array}$ 1 x 7 =

5. $\begin{array}{r} 9 \\ +6 \\ \hline \end{array}$ 9 x 6 =

6. $\begin{array}{r} 6 \\ +7 \\ \hline \end{array}$

7. $\begin{array}{r} 7 \\ +7 \\ \hline \end{array}$

8. $\begin{array}{r} 8 \\ +7 \\ \hline \end{array}$

Big Bears

Adult bears are very big. Add the numbers and circle the biggest number.

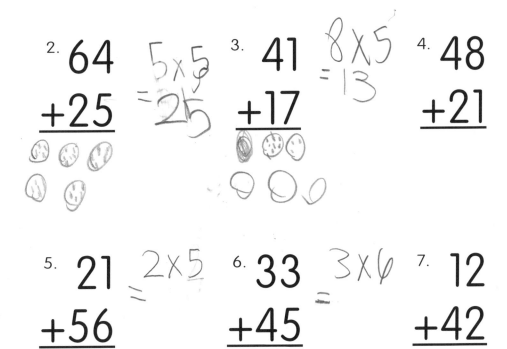

1.
$$55$$
$$+31$$

2.
$$64$$
$$+25$$

5x5
=25

3.
$$41$$
$$+17$$

8x5
=13

4.
$$48$$
$$+21$$

5.
$$21$$
$$+56$$

2x5

6.
$$33$$
$$+45$$

3x6

7.
$$12$$
$$+42$$

Page 4
1. 5   5. 6
2. 4   6. 3
3. 6   7. 2
4. 5   8. 6

Page 5
1. 5   5. 3
2. 5   6. 4
3. 7   7. 4
4. 2   8. 2

Page 6
1. ⑥   5. ⑥
2. 3   6. 5
3. 1   7. 5
4. 3   8. ⑦

Page 7

Flying High

Page 8
1. 6
2. 3
3. 6
4. 9

Page 9
1. 3   5. 5
2. 6   6. 5
3. 4   7. 4
4. 7   8. 8

Page 10
1. 8   5. 8
2. 4   6. 0
3. 7   7. 3
4. 4   8. 9

Page 11
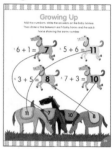

Page 12
1. 6   5. 8
2. 3   6. 7
3. 6   7. 4
4. 5   8. 1

Page 13
1. 9   5. 7
2. 5   6. 3
3. 8   7. 8
4. 6

Page 14
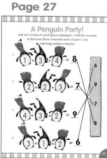
Cats Can Jump

Page 15
1. 2   5. 6
2. 4   6. 5
3. 9   7. 8
4. 1   8. 3

Page 16
1. 6
2. 4
3. 6
4. 5

Page 17
1. 9   5. 9
2. 6   6. 6
3. 7   7. 8
4. 4

Page 18
1. 6   5. 5
2. 6   6. ⑨
3. 8   7. 5
4. 7

Page 19
1. 7   5. 7
2. 5   6. 8
3. 6   7. 9
4. 4   8. 5

Page 20
1. 6   4. 8
2. 9   5. 8
3. 5   6. 7

Page 21
1. 7   5. 6
2. 9   6. 8
3. 5   7. 7
4. 6   8. 8

Page 22
1. 9   5. 7
2. 7   6. 7
3. 9   7. 4
4. 8   8. 9

Page 23

There are three
pairs of penguins.

Page 24
1. 8   5. 9
2. 5   6. 4
3. 9   7. 8
4. 6   8. 7

Page 25
1. 9   5. 4
2. 6   6. 7
3. 8   7. 4
4. 6   8. 8

Page 26
1. 9   5. 6
2. 7   6. 4
3. 8   7. 5
4. 7   8. 6

Page 27
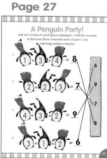
A Penguin Party!

Page 28
1. 6   5. 4
2. 8   6. 7
3. 8   7. 2
4. 9   8. 5

Page 29
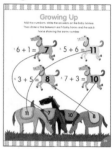
Growing Up

Page 30
1. 10   5. 10
2. 6   6. 11
3. 10   7. 8
4. 11

Page 31
1. 8   5. 11
2. 6   6. 10
3. 6   7. 8
4. 10

Page 32
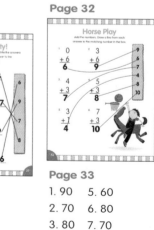
Horse Play

Page 33
1. 90   5. 60
2. 70   6. 80
3. 80   7. 70
4. 60   8. 40

Answer Key

Page 34

Page 35
1. 26	5. 89
2. 65	6. 67
3. 86	7. 87
4. 58	8. 68

Page 36
1. 88	5. 89
2. 59	6. 66
3. 96	7. 89
4. 82	8. 97

Page 37

Doggie Dance

Page 38
2. 1 + 1 = _2_
3. 4 + 4 = _8_
4. 5 + 5 = _10_
5. 6 + 6 = _12_
6. 2 + 2 = _4_
7. 3 + 3 = _6_
8. 8 + 8 = _16_

Page 39
1. 88	5. 79
2. 49	6. 54
3. 78	7. 64
4. 76	

Page 40
1. 6
2. 8
3. 7
4. 9

Page 41
1. 69
2. 93
3. (99)
4. 58
5. 87
6. 73

Page 42
1. 79	5. (107)
2. 99	6. 67
3. 75	7. 98
4. 63	8. 42

Page 43
1. 57¢
2. 16¢

Page 44
1. 11	5. 10
2. 12	6. 12
3. 14	7. 12
4. 11	

Page 45

Page 46
1. 12	5. 15
2. 12	6. 14
3. 10	7. 15
4. 13	8. 16

Page 47
1. 12	5. 16
2. 11	6. 13
3. 17	7. 10
4. 13	8. 13

Page 48

Funky Monkeys

Page 49
1. 18
2. 16
3. 11

Page 50
1. 16	5. 14
2. 15	6. 11
3. 12	7. 12
4. 17	8. 13

Page 51
1. 13	5. 13
2. 12	6. 16
3. 13	7. 10
4. 15	8. 17

Page 52
1. 16	5. 12
2. 12	6. (10)
3. 14	7. 16
4. 13	8. 11

Page 53

Litter of Mice

Page 54
1. 16	5. 15
2. 17	6. 18
3. 13	7. 10
4. 11	8. 11

Page 55
1. 10
2. 16
3. 17
4. 11
5. 14
6. 14

Page 56
1. 14	5. 11
2. 18	6. 12
3. 17	7. 13
4. 15	8. 11

Page 57
1. 18	5. 12
2. 12	6. 13
3. 11	7. 10
4. 13	8. 14

Page 58

Baby Bears

Page 59
1. 12	5. 16
2. 11	6. 13
3. 13	7. 16
4. 13	8. (10)

Page 60
1. 18	5. 15
2. 11	6. 13
3. 16	7. 14
4. 12	8. 15

Page 61
1. 86	5. 77
2. (89)	6. 78
3. 58	7. 54
4. 69	

Good work,

_____ !

(Name)

You did a great job practicing your addition!